DRAWING

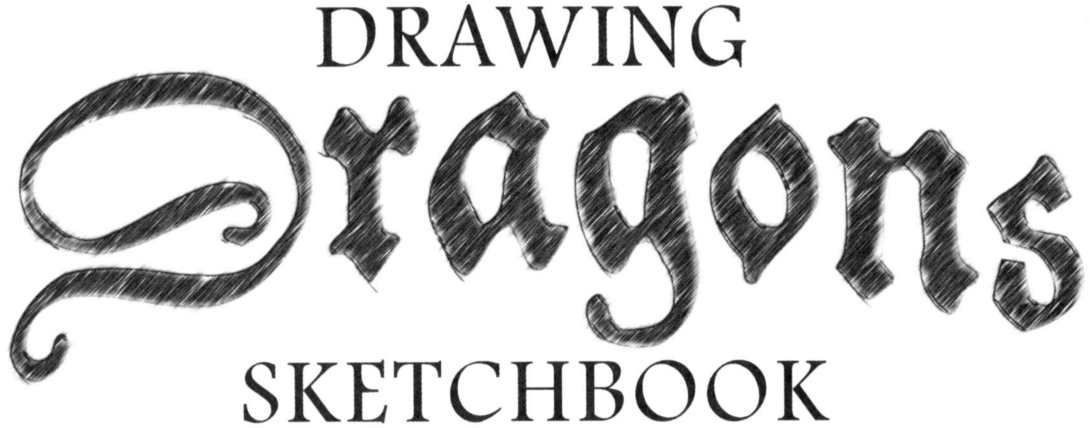

SKETCHBOOK

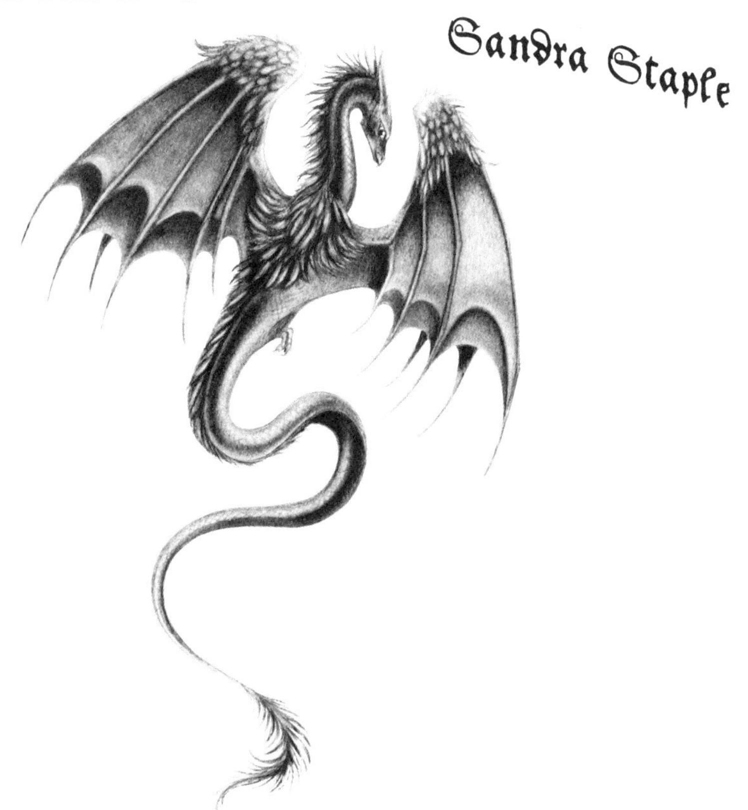

An Artist's Notebook for Creating and Illustrating Your Own Dragon Art

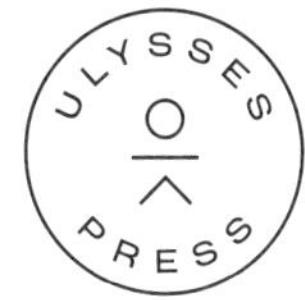

Published in the United States by:
Ulysses Press
PO Box 3440
Berkeley, CA 94703
www.ulyssespress.com

ISBN: 978-1-64604-242-5

Printed in the United States by Kingery Printing Company
10 9 8 7 6 5 4 3 2 1

Acquisitions editor: Ashten Evans
Managing editor: Claire Chun
Editor: Barbara Schultz
Proofreader: Janet Vail
Front cover design: Jake Flaherty
Cover and interior art: Sandra Staple

This Book Belongs To

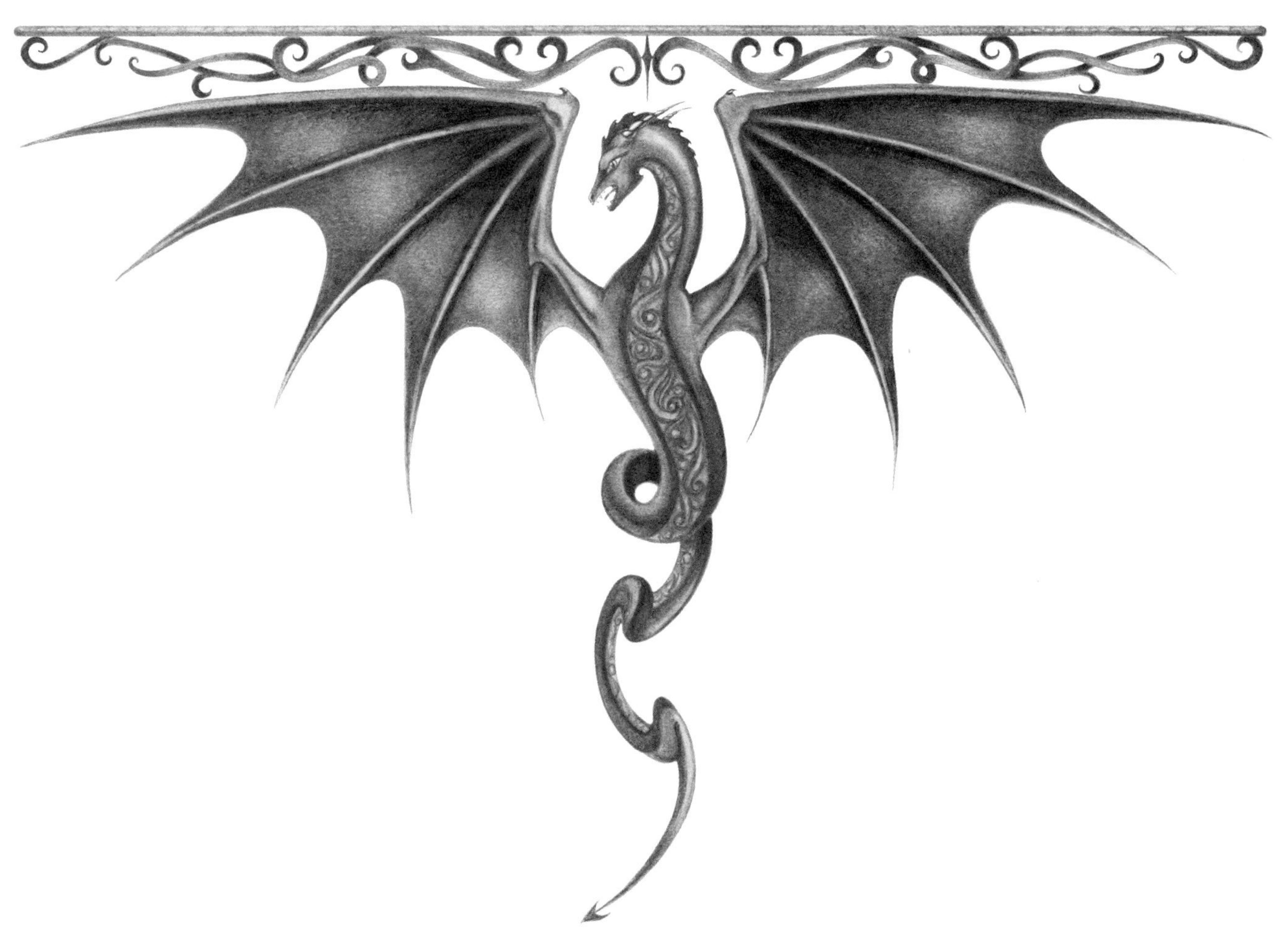

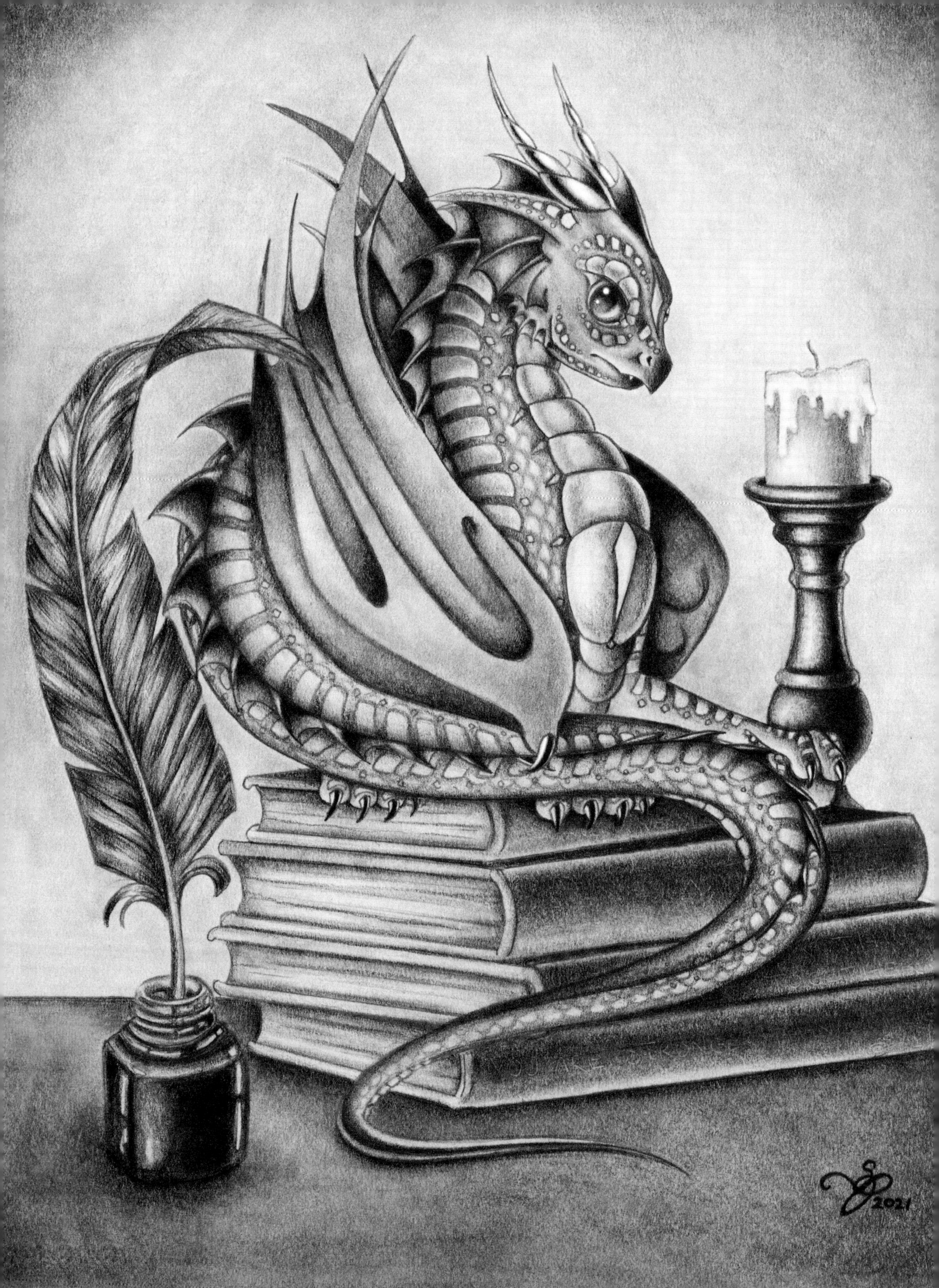
2021

Introduction

So you've come here to draw dragons, have you? I will assume this is the case as otherwise you may have been more inclined to pick up a sketchbook on drawing horses, or robots, or robot horses, or any other thing that catches your fancy.

Well, I'm here to tell you that the joke is on you! Okay... yes, the title of the book *does* say it is a *Drawing Dragons Sketchbook,* and there are, quite conveniently, several dragon drawing tutorials at the beginning of this sketchbook to start you on your fierce, fire-breathing-beast-drawing adventure, but you may have also noticed something: This sketchbook is full of blank pages! Without a single dragon on them! Yes, yes, there are also lots of pages *with* dragons on them, but never mind those. Pay attention to the blank ones—the ones that you get to fill with your art. This book also has a spot where you can write your name as the owner of this sketchbook. You know what this means, right? You don't actually have to draw dragons in it at all! It's yours! Draw whatever you want! But of course, if you *choose* to draw dragons in it, it certainly does seem like the *perfect* sketchbook to do so in. Either way, you are the owner of this book, so draw whatever you like and just enjoy the fact that it is your art—your own masterpieces adorning its pages. Don't fret if your drawings don't all turn out perfect. They are your creations, and you will only get better with practice and time.

That is what I want you to take away here: This is your book, with a little bit of content in it from me to you, just to get you started. Don't worry about what anyone else says you should or shouldn't draw. Draw what you love, and you will love what you draw.

GETTING STARTED: SUPPLIES AND DRAWING MEDIA

Drawing is a wonderful, relaxing hobby, and can be a fairly inexpensive one as well. There are some basic supplies you will need to get started, so let's take a look at the bare minimum.

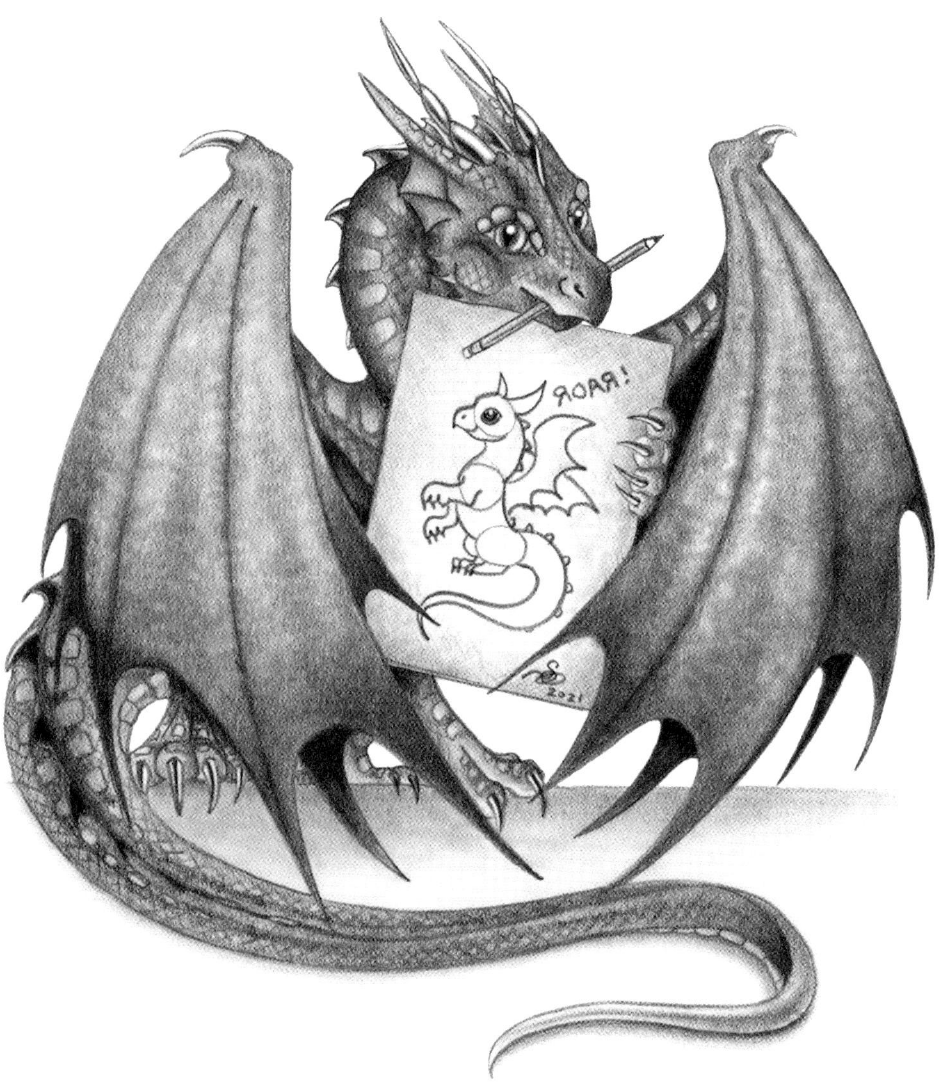

SKETCHBOOK: Looks like you've got that one covered! I always recommend picking up a nice sketchbook if you can, something with smooth white paper in it. Make sure the paper is acid- and lignin-free or your paper will yellow over time, and make sure there are no lines on the paper.

> TIP: I've had people tell me they like drawing on lined paper as they use the lines as a guide. If this is the case for you, try getting some darkly lined loose-leaf to put under your blank page, or even print one with black lines on a printer. You should be able to see the lines enough to use them as a guide, without the lines ruining your drawing.

SCRAP PAPER: I like to keep regular printer paper around for rough sketching. Don't use this paper for your finished artwork, though. It warps easily and turns really yellow after even just a couple of years!

GRAPHITE PENCILS: Get yourself a nice set of drawing pencils. Graphite pencils are most commonly graded using the HB system, which indicates the degree of hardness or blackness; the letter H indicates how hard a pencil is, while the letter B is used to indicate how black the pencil's mark will be (which usually means the lead is also much softer). HB is the middle ground, while an F pencil is a special one with a type of lead that can keep a finer point. So the higher the number on an H pencil, the harder the pencil is, and the higher the number on a B pencil, the darker it is.

The main pencils I use are F, B, and 2B for drawing, then 4B and 6B for shading really dark areas. I don't personally like using H pencils for drawing, as they are harder and dent the paper, which is annoying to shade over.

ERASERS: I like to use the white rectangle gum erasers for large areas and an electric eraser for small areas. The electric erasers are really neat, but be careful if the eraser part at the end gets too short. The metal part that holds the eraser nub will scratch up your paper if you let the eraser part get too short!

PENCIL SHARPENER: Regular, old-fashioned hand sharpeners that have a little compartment to store the shavings are the best. Replace them whenever they get dull so they don't eat your pencils!

SMUDGE STICKS/BLENDING STUMPS: These are just tightly rolled up sticks of paper, but they work great for smudging graphite pencil and other black-and-white media.

LIGHT TABLE/TRACING LIGHT PAD: This is a great tool for tracing your drawings onto new paper, and you can buy them online for less than twenty dollars. If you don't want to shell out the cash for one, you can get the same effect by holding your drawing up to a window on a sunny day.

DRAWING MEDIA: There are lots of wonderful drawing media to choose from other than graphite pencil, such as charcoal, chalk, pastel, colored pencil, pen, and more.

Like graphite pencil, **charcoal** is another black-and-white medium that's fun to work with. Charcoal is usually used for less precise, quick drawings; it's popular to use when planning out large paintings and murals because it is soft and easy to erase and smudge. **Chalk** is very similar to work with but offers more color variation in light, muted tones. One downside to drawing with these media is that you will need some sort of fixative spray to protect your art from being smudged or damaged when you are finished.

While not typically very precise, **oil pastels** offer vibrant colors and the ability to smudge and blend colors. Artist-quality **colored pencils** are my personal favorite, as they offer a full, vivid color range. With the option to buy colored pencils with either soft or hard leads, you can achieve very precise details and also wonderful color blending.

Drawing with **pens** and **markers** is fun but not for the faint of heart—there is no erasing your mistakes if you make any! That being said, high-quality gel pens can do a fairly decent job at covering up and hiding small errors and come in lots of wonderful colors.

So which drawing medium to choose? This sketchbook will focus on drawing and shading using graphite pencils, because that is the cheapest and easiest medium to use and obtain a great level of detail with. That being said, I encourage you to try some of the other drawing media to get a feel for what you like best!

My first book, *Drawing Dragons*, is also all drawn in graphite pencil (with a color insert featuring dragons drawn in colored pencil), while my second book, *Drawing Fantastic Dragons*, is entirely done in colored pencil, and the tutorials there include steps on coloring each dragon, which might be helpful if you are interested in drawing and coloring dragons in colored pencil.

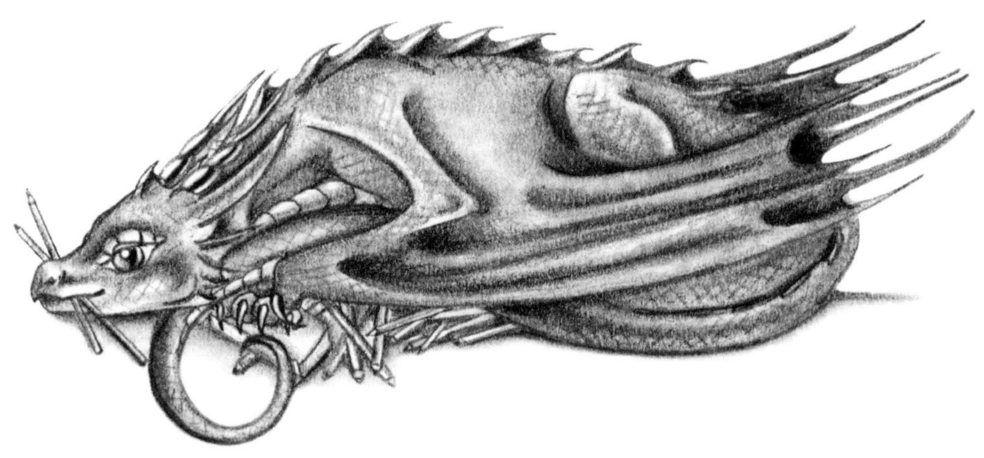

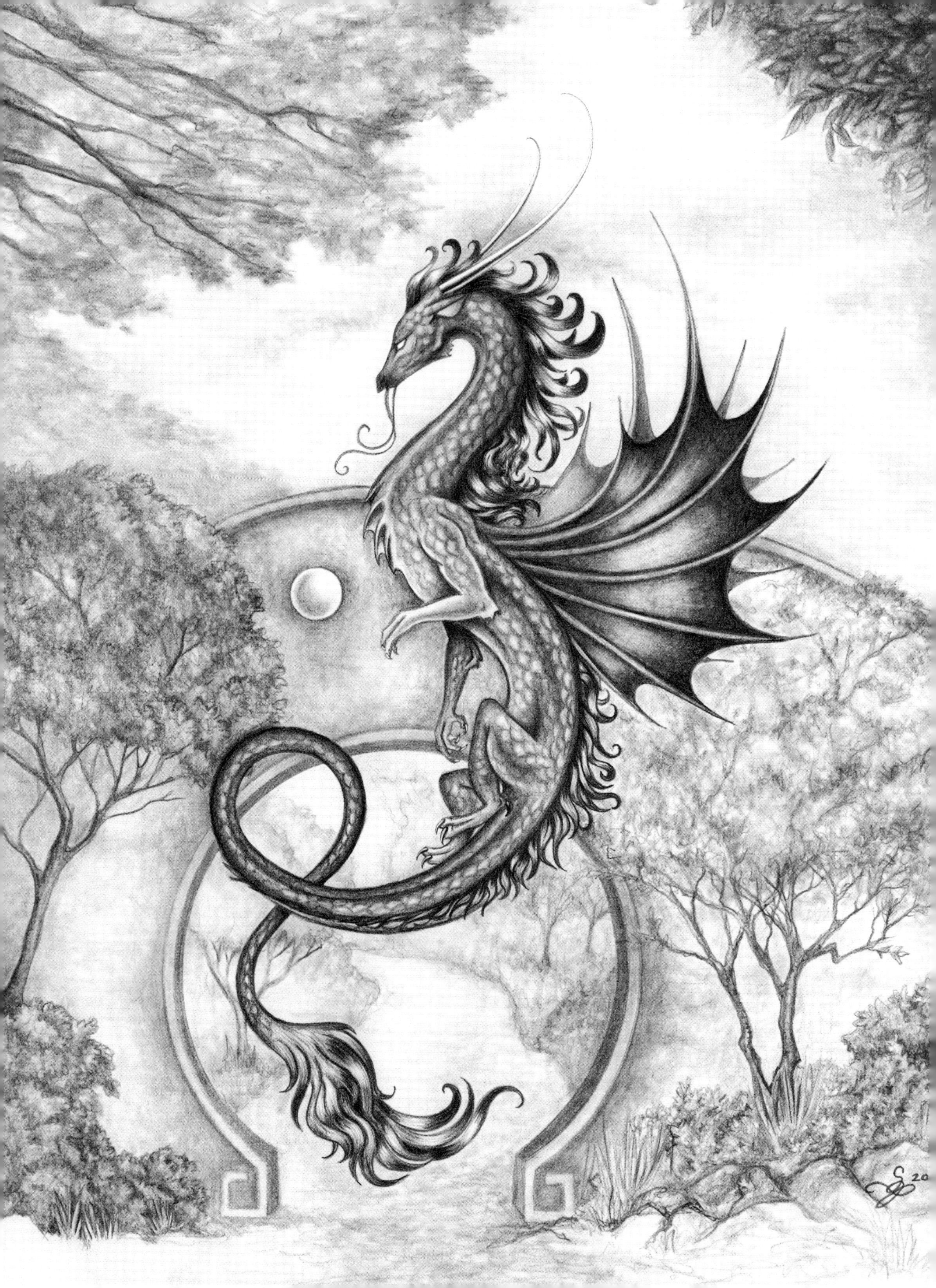

Drawing Dragons Demonstrations

Well I suppose since this *is,* after all, a drawing dragons sketchbook, we should actually look at drawing some dragons!

Dragons are complicated creatures, and there are so many different types. I don't have room in this sketchbook to get into all the unique parts of dragons you can draw and how to customize them. If I did that, there would be no room for your own sketches, and both of my previous drawing dragon books *(Drawing Dragons* and *Drawing Fantastic Dragons)* do that already! If you enjoy these tutorials, you'll be glad to know that I do not repeat any of the same lessons between the books, so you can enjoy all three of them and have lots of different dragon drawings to try.

This is just a short lesson to get you started. Remember that there is no "right or wrong" way to draw a dragon—that is the great thing about drawing mythical creatures! These are simply guidelines to point you in the right direction, and from there, you get to draw your own dragons however you like! Don't give up on your drawings if they don't go the way you want the first time. Learning to draw well takes time and practice.

Finally, I've included some little bonus drawings throughout the actual sketchbook section of this book, to keep you inspired. You can enjoy them as is, incorporate them into your own art, or color them if you want to! I am going to color them myself and put videos online of the process, so visit @SandraStaple on social media to find the videos and follow along if you like.

Above all, just enjoy the process of creating art! And remember, if some of your drawings don't turn out the way you want, don't be too hard on yourself. That is just part of learning to draw, and it happens to every artist. The more you practice, the more you will improve, and you'll be proud of yourself when you do!

DRAWING A DRAGON'S HEAD

The most important feature of any animal drawing, in my opinion, is the head. The rest of the body can look great but if the head, face, or eyes are "off," it can ruin the entire drawing. So let's take a look at drawing a classic dragon head first.

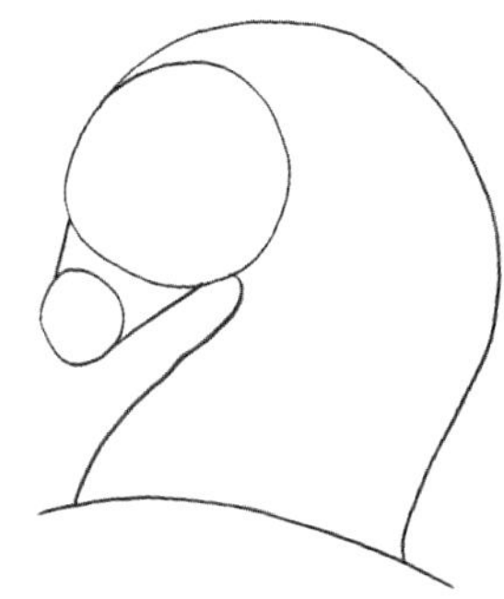

1 I always start the head out with one large circle that I call the main "skull" circle. I then draw another smaller circle for the snout and attach it to the skull circle with two lines. The farther away the second circle is, the longer your dragon's head will be. Then attach the neck near the top of the skull circle and make it curve gracefully down—this will give your dragon a nice, arching neck. This is your basic dragon head shape.

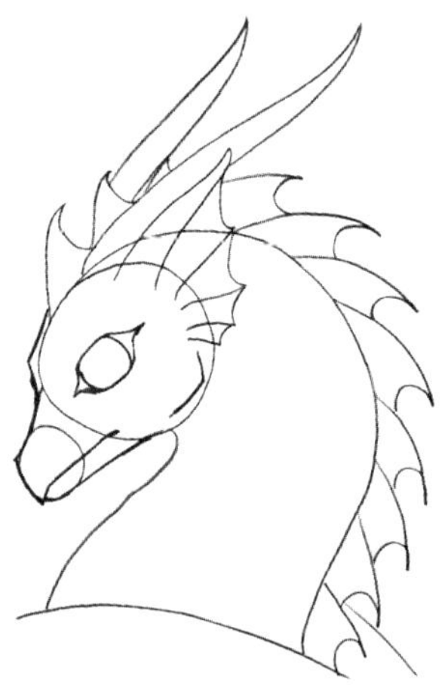

2 Once you have the basic shape, you can start building some details. I usually start shaping out the nose and mouth first, and then the eye ridge. Then I'll figure out where the eye should go. (Hint: a larger eye works well for smaller dragons, and a smaller eye is better for really big dragons.) Next draw in an ear and figure out where the jaw ends. Last step is to decide what type of spines or horns you want your dragon to have.

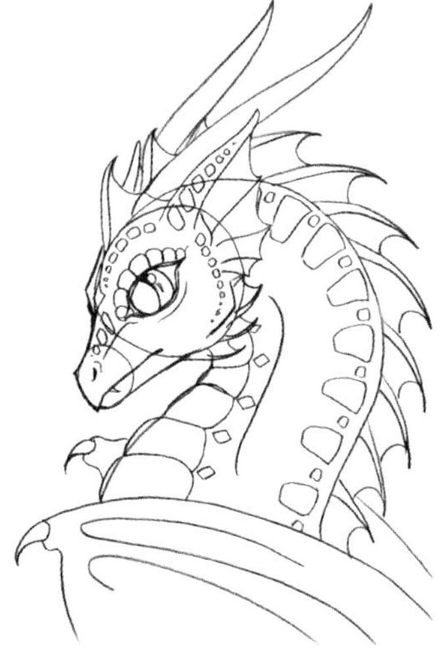

3 Now that you have the basic features sketched out, you can flesh out all the details! I always start with the eye first. Add the type of pupil you want, and any eye ridges. Give your dragon a nostril and maybe some teeth. Add some scales or patterns and belly plates if you like. I decided to make a pattern along this dragon's neck, and draw a bit of his wing showing.

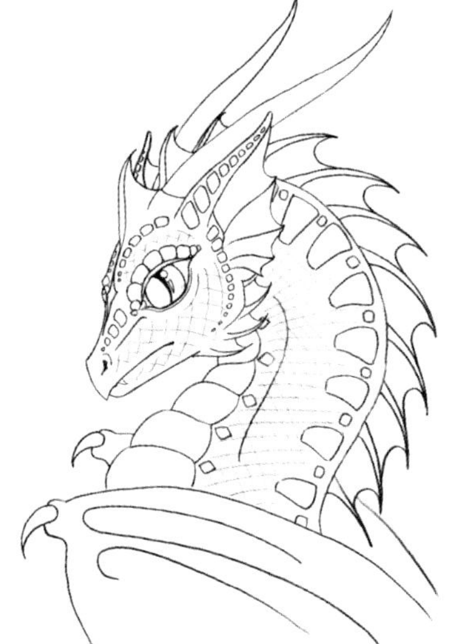

4 Now that you have fleshed out all the details in the last step, you can either erase your building lines or copy your drawing onto a new piece of paper. Once the building lines from the circles are gone, add some very light lines for scales, as these will help in the next step when you begin shading.

5 Start your shading with a B pencil (or HB if you don't have one), and don't press too hard in this step! Here, as you can see, I have rounded out each scale, using the grid I drew in Step 4 as a guide. Make sure to leave the middle scales going down the neck white; you can use that later to make the neck appear curved and muscular.

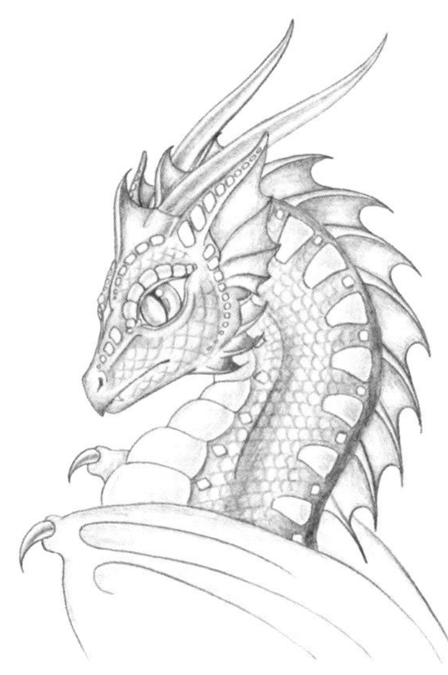

6 This next step was done using only a blending stump—no pencil at all! I used a small, thin one so it was easy to blend between the tighter spaces. As you can see, it both darkens the drawing and flattens it a bit at the same time, but the idea is just to smooth everything out and use the graphite pencil already on the paper to fill in the white areas.

7 Once the blending is done, it's time to finish up the drawing by darkening in the shadows and any other areas you want to have more contrast. I darkened certain areas to highlight muscles and bone structure on this dragon using a 2B pencil.

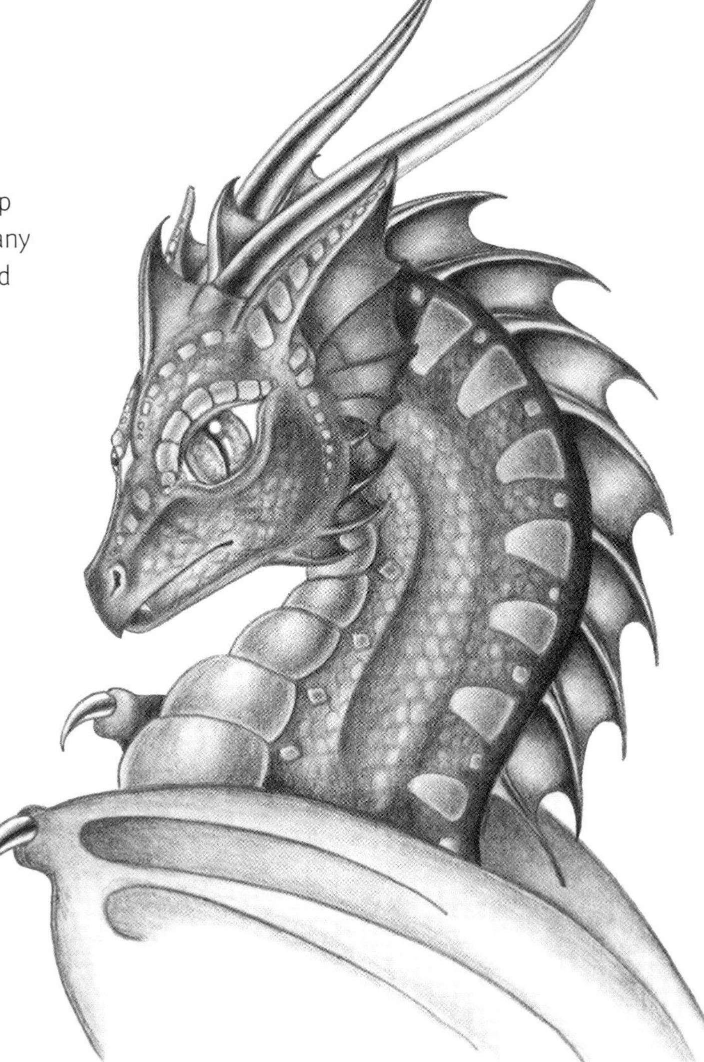

DRAWING A LONG, LEAN, EASTERN DRAGON

Now that you have learned to draw a dragon's head, it's time to draw an entire dragon! Let's start by drawing a dragon that doesn't have any wings—an Eastern dragon—so that you can concentrate on drawing the body and limbs.

1 Whenever I draw any type of dragon, I start by drawing what I call the basic body shape. This is going to be a long, lean dragon, so the basic body shape is going to be very serpent-like. Start with the head exactly the way you did in the previous tutorial. Because this is a long, lean dragon, the neck is quite long and is going to curve down to another large circle for the chest. Continue with more curving lines off the chest circle until you get to where you think it makes sense to put the dragon's hind legs; draw a small circle here for the dragon's rump. After that, all the remaining curving lines are just tail!

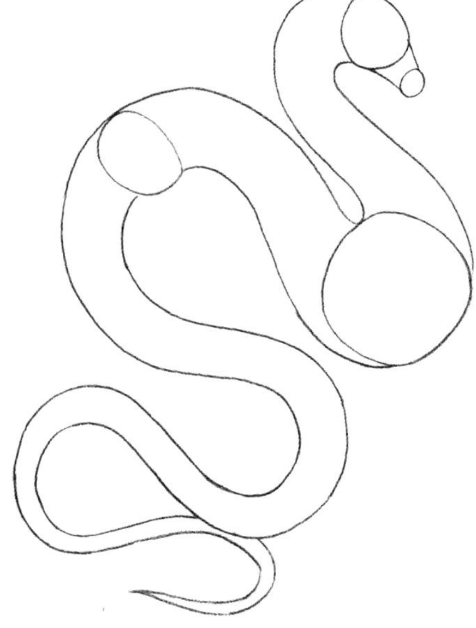

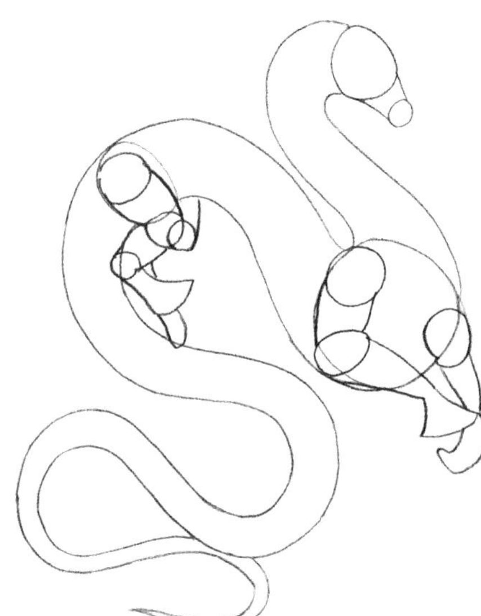

2 Next, figure out where you want to put this guy's arms and legs! Start by drawing small circles for the shoulders, and another similarly sized circle for the elbow and connect them. Draw tapering lines down to where the claws will go, and then just draw a generic shape for the claws; for one I drew a fan-shape, as that claw will be stretched out, while the other shape is curved like a kidney bean. Follow similar steps for the back legs.

3 Now that the dragon's basic shape and limbs are laid out, you can place the eye and ear and add horns if you want. You can decide how the dragon's features should look. For example, I decided to give this guy antler-like horns and a thick, furry mane and tail.

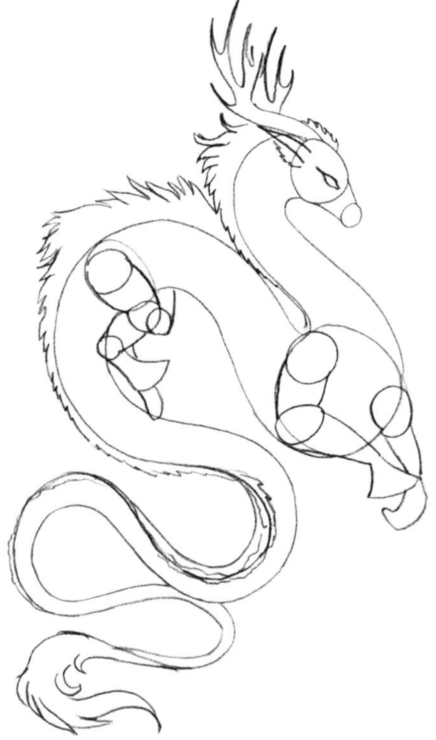

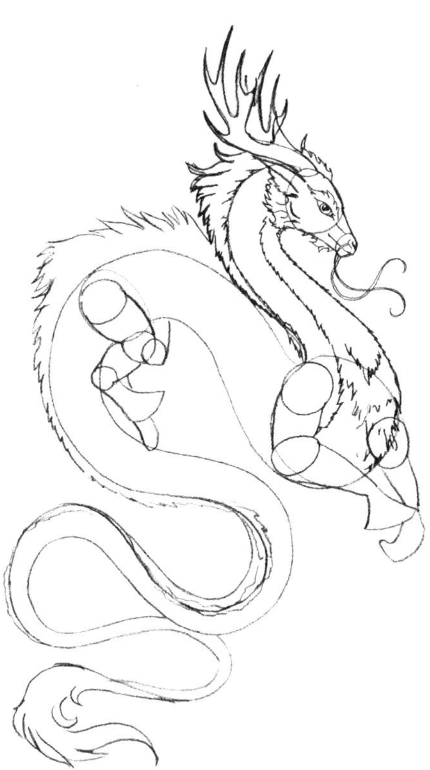

4 Once all the basic pieces are drawn, you can start sketching out the details, starting with the head. Draw in the details for the eye and nose. Because this guy is an Eastern dragon, I'm going to have his nostril actually wrap around the front of his snout and give him some long whiskers. Add a bit of a beard to the end of his face. Finally, make his belly and underside furry as well.

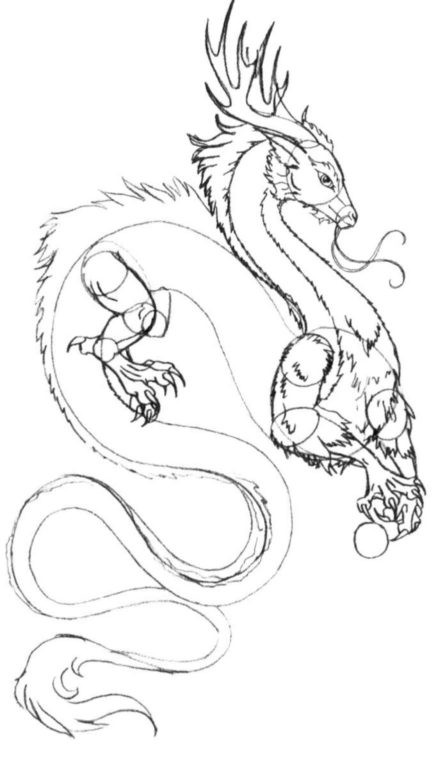

5 The next step is to draw the legs and claws. Claws can be really challenging, so don't be discouraged if they are difficult for you! It can help to use another image as a reference, too. Cat claws, in particular, make a good model. Start by erasing the bottom of the fan and the bean shape you drew for each claw, and then draw the fingers and toes.

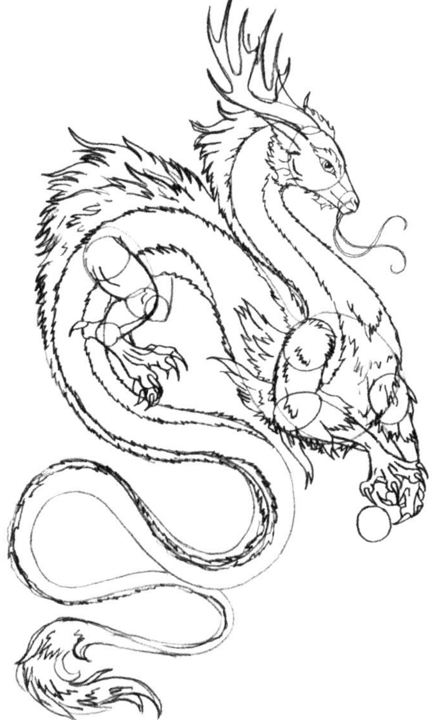

6 Now that the face and limbs are done, you can fill in the rest of the details. Give this guy a bit of long fur coming off the back of his arms since he doesn't have wings, and then make the fur on his back a bit longer. Continue his furry underside all the way down his tail.

7 Copy your drawing onto new paper or erase your building lines. Once they are gone, draw in a light grid for his scales. Don't press very hard when drawing this grid! You are going to draw each scale out, so the grid is just there so that the curved scales will follow a pattern.

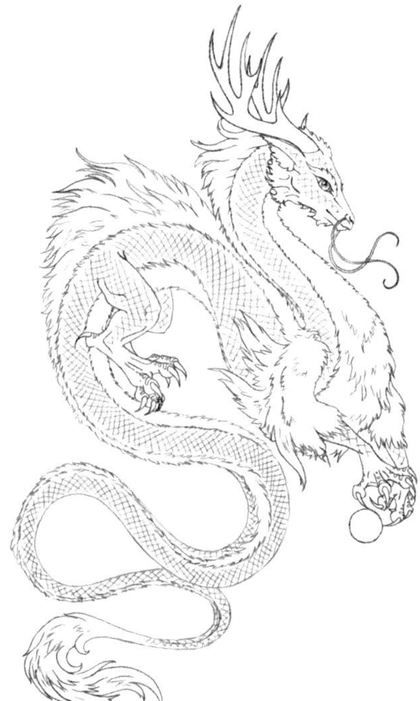

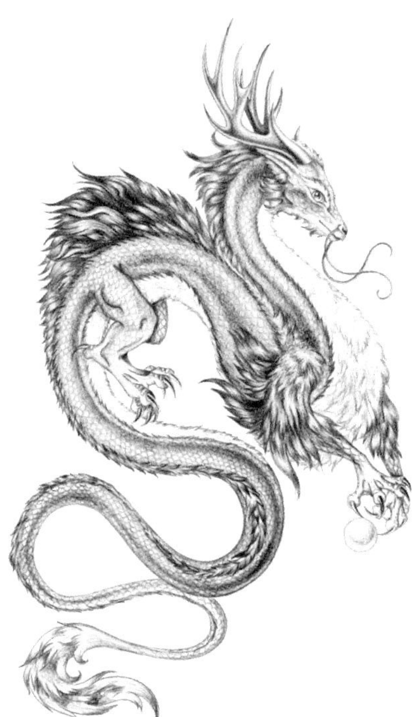

8 Time to start shading! I recommend using a B pencil for this step. Start with the head, and make sure you use a piece of scrap paper to cover up the parts of the drawing that you aren't working on so that you don't smudge it with your hand and make a mess of your paper. Draw each scale out like a rounded fish scale, and add darker shading in the middle down his neck, body, and tail to round him out. Keep his belly light in color, but make his furry ridge dark. Make the fur look shiny by leaving it white in the middle, but darker on both ends.

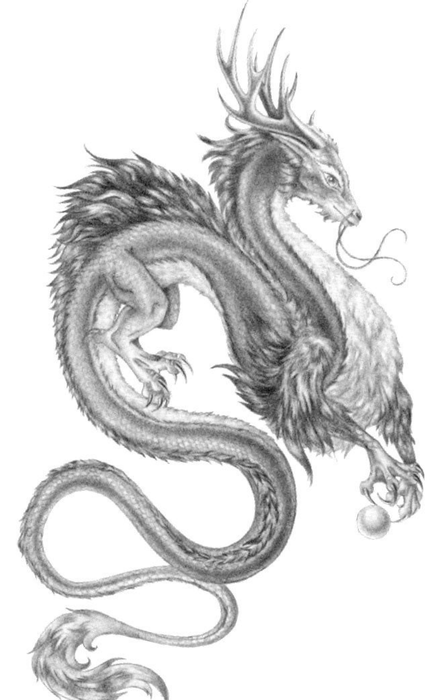

9 This step is done entirely with a blending stump. I like to blend and smudge my drawings, because I think it smooths everything out, and works well for shading lighter areas such as the claws and belly fur, but it's up to you whether to use blending and smudging on yours.

10 Now that the blending is done, you just need to darken the shadows and highlights in this dragon's fur and add a background! While Eastern dragons can have many different powers, they most commonly have powers over the weather and bodies of water, such as oceans, lakes, or rivers, so I'm going to draw this wise dragon serenely guarding his river home, but you can add any type of background you like!

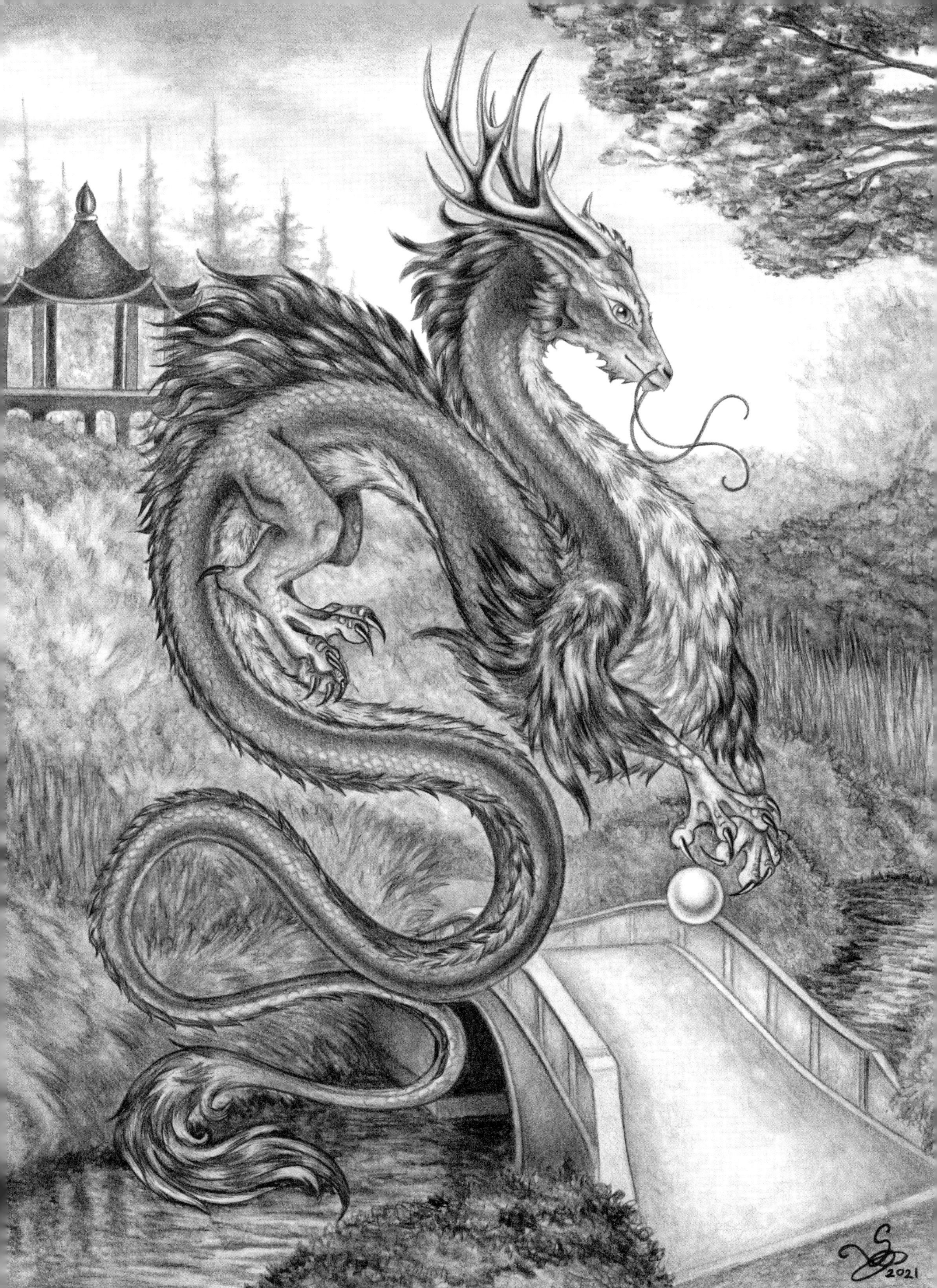

DRAWING A STOCKY, WESTERN DRAGON

You just finished drawing an Eastern dragon with a long slinky body type. Next, try drawing a big, broad Western dragon! Now you can add wings to your beast. In order for you to get some practice drawing classic, bat-like, dragon wings, I'll show you how to draw them fully extended.

1 Once again, you'll start with the basic body shape, but this time it won't be nearly as long. Start with the head as you did before, but because this dragon is stocky, the neck isn't going to be nearly as long as the Eastern dragon's. Draw a nice large circle for the chest, and draw the rump circle much closer to the chest circle than last time (while still allowing some room between.) Though Western dragons can have very long tails, for starters you are going to draw a shorter one. (You'll see why in Step 4.)

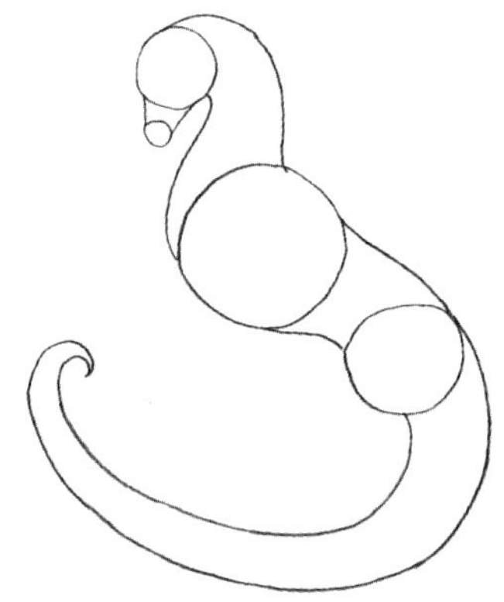

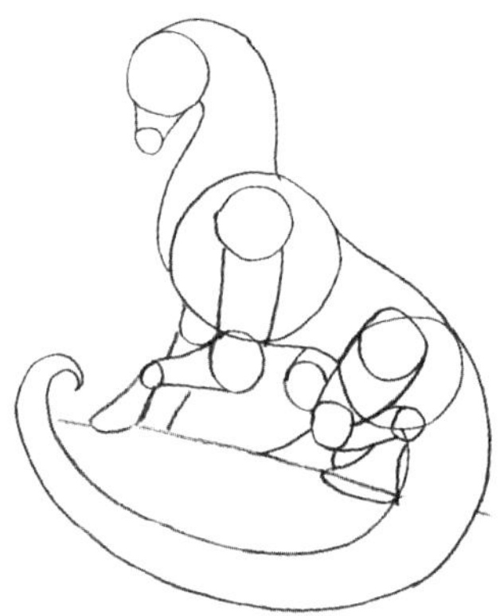

2 Drawing the arms and legs for a Western dragon is very much the same as in the Eastern dragon tutorial, except the Western dragon's limbs are usually a bit larger and better for walking on with long strides. I think of Eastern dragon legs and claws as being more of a mix between bird and lizard legs (you can almost picture them slinking along the ground), whereas Western dragon legs have a weird mix of human-horse-dog-cat-alligator features. Luckily, just their legs and claws are like that; it would be weird if their faces were like that too!

3 Wings are often an important feature for classic Western dragons! Although these appendages are technically a third set of limbs, they share a lot in common with arms and should attach at the shoulders. Draw the wing "arms" similar to actual arms, but much longer and thinner. From each wing's "wrist," you can draw three or four spines (almost like long fingers). I usually add another spine coming from the wing's elbow as well, and then attach all the spines with curving lines.

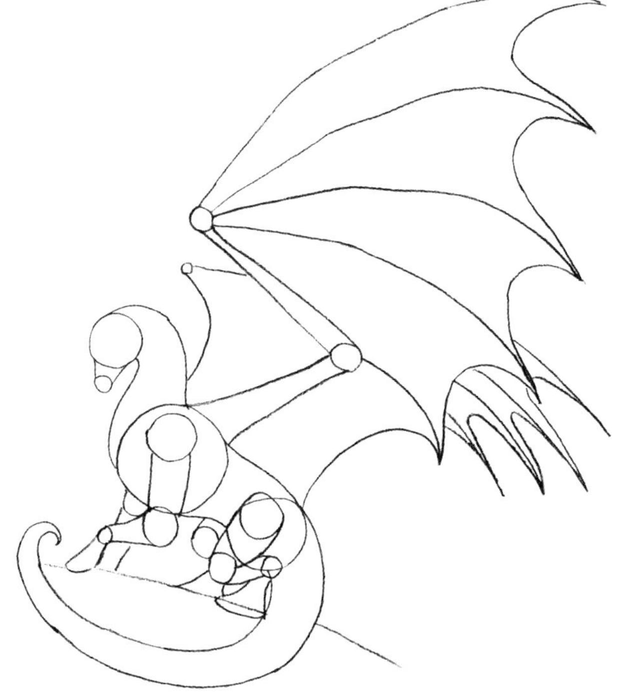

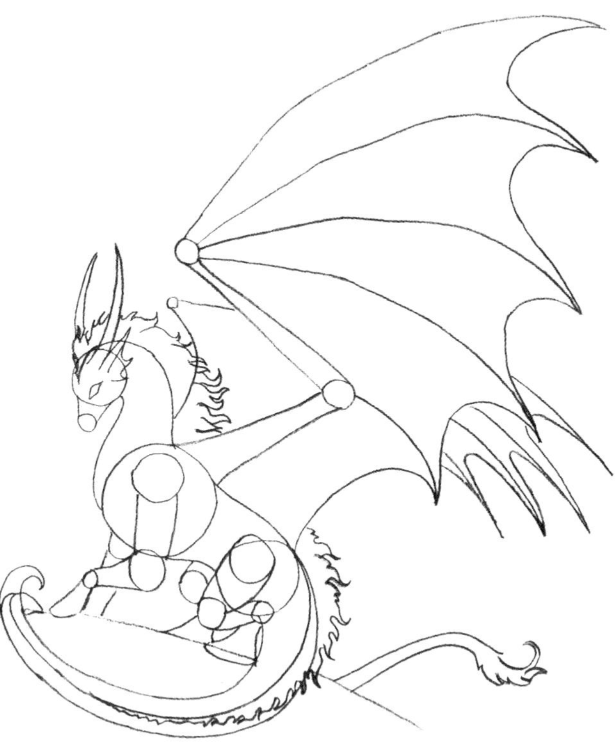

4 I didn't actually want this dragon to have a short tail, but I wanted to have it disappear and reappear behind the rocks she is standing on. Now that I've placed the legs, I can rough in the ground and the place where her tail will come out. This dragon will have a long, wavy, hair-like spine. You can also add ears and horns and place the eye.

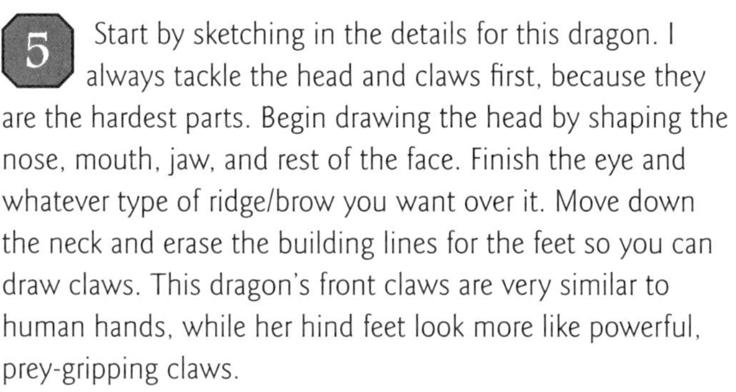

5 Start by sketching in the details for this dragon. I always tackle the head and claws first, because they are the hardest parts. Begin drawing the head by shaping the nose, mouth, jaw, and rest of the face. Finish the eye and whatever type of ridge/brow you want over it. Move down the neck and erase the building lines for the feet so you can draw claws. This dragon's front claws are very similar to human hands, while her hind feet look more like powerful, prey-gripping claws.

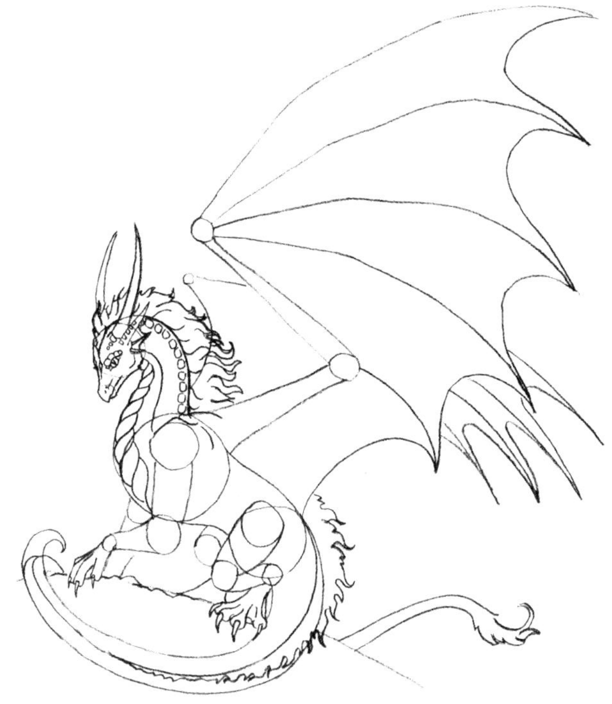

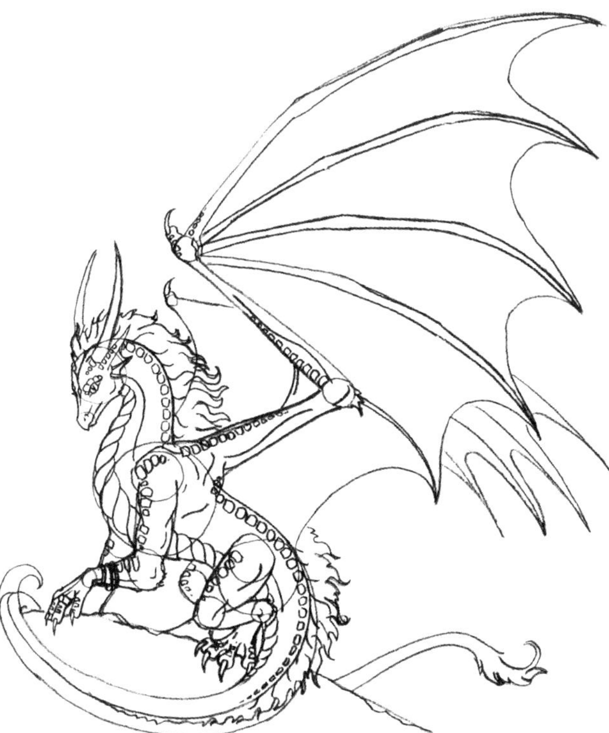

6 Add a thumb-like claw to the top of the wing, and draw another line along each spine in the wing if you want to make them thicker and even more finger-like. Then finish up your dragon by adding any remaining details, such as belly scales or muscular definition to the legs and arms. I also decided to add a bit of a blocky scale pattern to her body along the spine and the edges of her limbs.

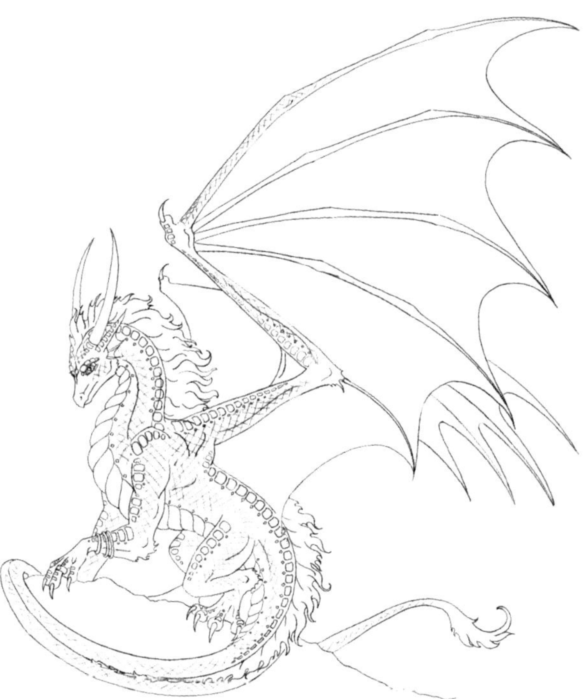

7 Now that all the sketching is done, it's time to clean up the drawing and get ready to shade it! For this detailed drawing, I definitely wanted to copy it onto a new piece of paper. When I was a teenager, I always used my bedroom window to trace drawings onto a new piece of paper, so don't worry if you don't have a light table.

8 I started shading in the top right corner of the wings because I'm left-handed, but you can start shading wherever you like—just make sure you have a piece of scrap paper to put over your drawing so you don't smudge it as you go. I used an HB pencil this time and made light, circular scribbles to shade in the wings. Don't worry if you can see a bit of the lines in the wings, as this will give the membranes a bit of texture.

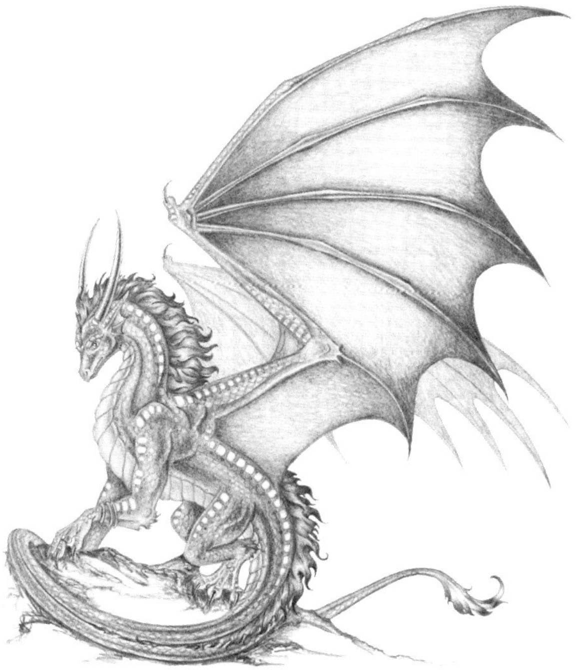

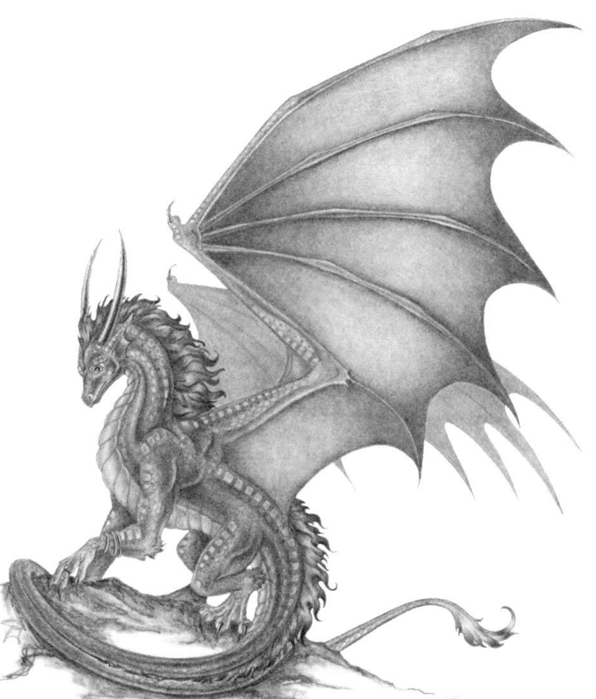

9 This is the blending step, and I find it works really well to fill in the wings. It smooths them out really nicely while still allowing a bit of texture to show through. I also used the blending stump to add a bit of shading to her pattern, and to the rocks she is standing on.

10 Our dragon is looking pretty good after the last step, but she needs some of the shadows to be darkened. You can also use an electric eraser to lighten areas that might be too dark, such as in her hair. Finally, add a background that suits your beast! Historically, Western dragons have often been depicted fighting knights, raiding castles, or guarding treasure, but you can draw them doing pretty much anything you want. Maybe this dragon is just waiting to meet up with some of her friends to go for a leisurely flight... and perhaps crash a castle party while they're at it!

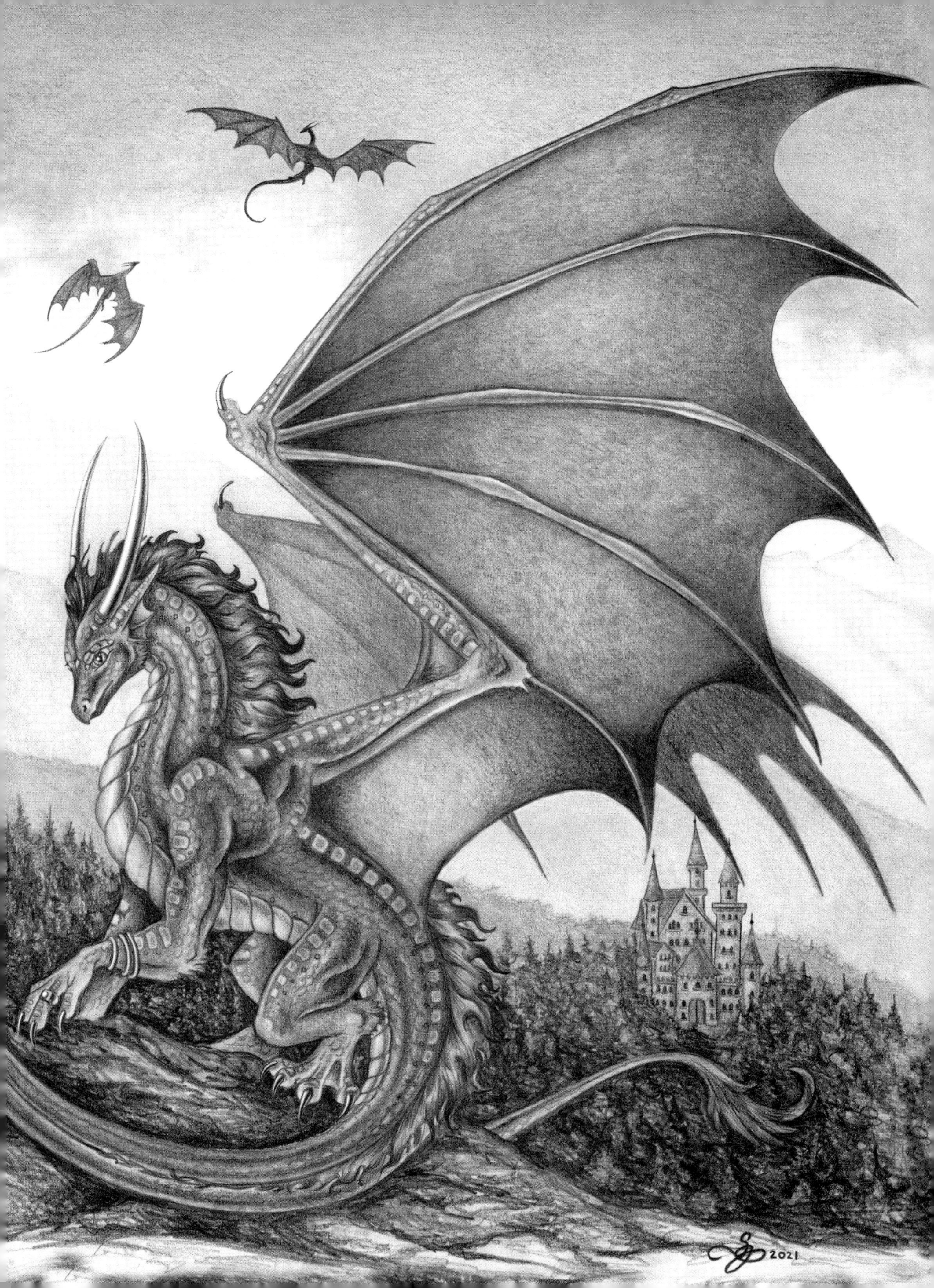

DRAWING A MINIATURE DRAGON

We've looked at drawing a long, lean Eastern dragon and a stocky, muscular Western dragon, so let's take a look at a third dragon body type—that of a compact, miniature dragon. Drawing a small dragon is very similar to drawing a large dragon, except the proportions are a bit different. It's like drawing an eagle versus a sparrow; everything on the little creature is smaller in proportion to its body size—except the head! Usually, the legs, arms, tail, and wings will all be a bit shorter in comparison to a full-size Western dragon, but the head will be larger. Follow these steps to see what I mean.

1 Start again by drawing your basic dragon form. This step is going to be very similar in proportions to drawing a stocky dragon, but with a smaller chest circle. You might also want to draw the nose circle closer to or right up against the skull circle if you want your dragon's face to be cute. If you want your dragon to be small, but not overly cute, make the face longer by doing the opposite.

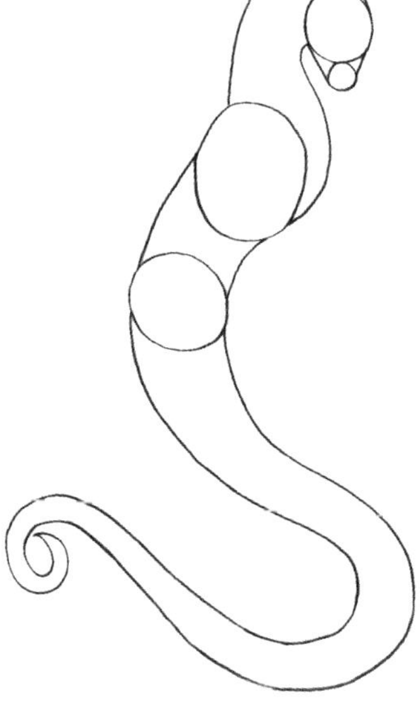

2 Decide how you want to place the legs and arms. In this case, you are going to draw this dragon landing on a branch, so draw the arms and legs reaching out. Make sure they are not too long! Draw fan-like shapes for the front claws for now, but try to draw a somewhat foot-like shape for the bottom two. You can flesh these out more later.

3 Draw the wings. You already drew some fully stretched out wings, so make these wings curve in, like the dragon is swooping its wings down for a landing. This is my favorite way to draw wings, because it's easier to fit everything onto the paper and can be more interesting.

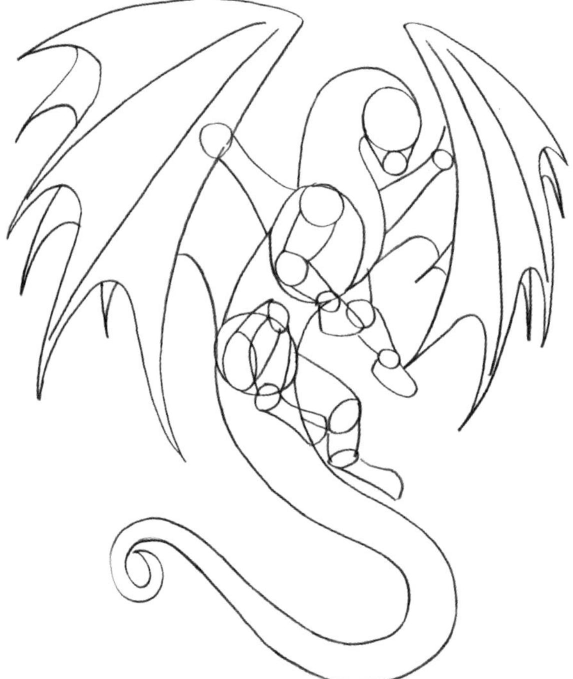

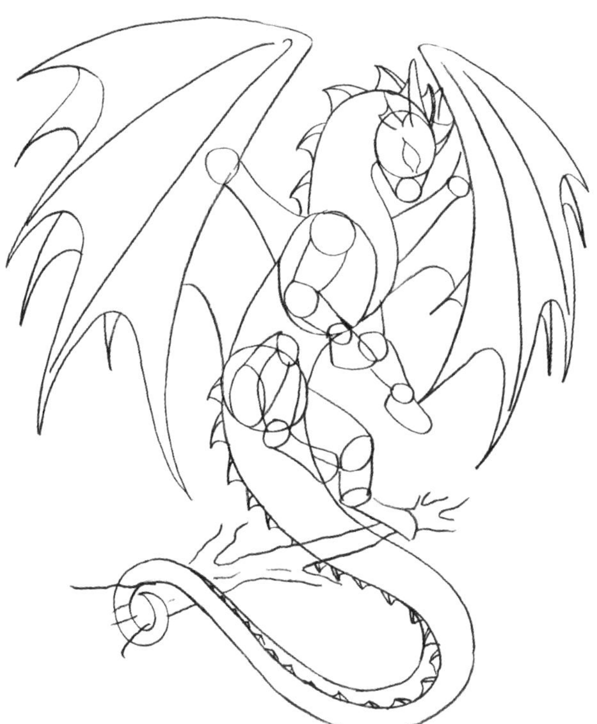

4 Figure out what remaining details you want to add to your basic layout and place the eye. Will your dragon have horns or spikes; ears or no ears? I'm giving this dragon classic curved spikes going down its neck and back, and simple little ears, but no horns this time, as they seem like they would be less practical for little tree-dragons. (We wouldn't want them getting tangled up in the branches!)

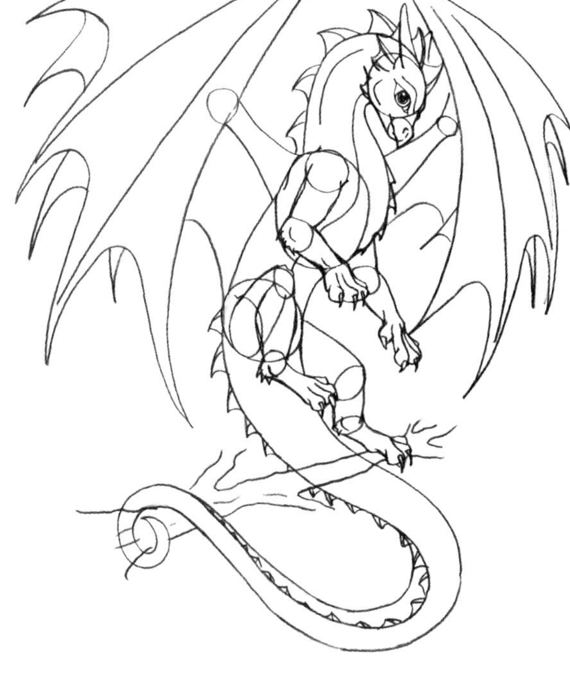

5 It's time to start sketching in the details! Start with the head and face by drawing in the shape of the nose, mouth, and jaw, and finishing the eye. If you want your dragon to look more cute and gentle, give it a big round pupil. If you want it to look more lizard-like, draw a long, thin slit similar to the eye in the head tutorial earlier. Shape the arms and legs to give them some muscle tone, and then erase the end of the feet shapes so you can draw in claws. Because this dragon is little, its claws are smaller too—almost like a house cat's paws.

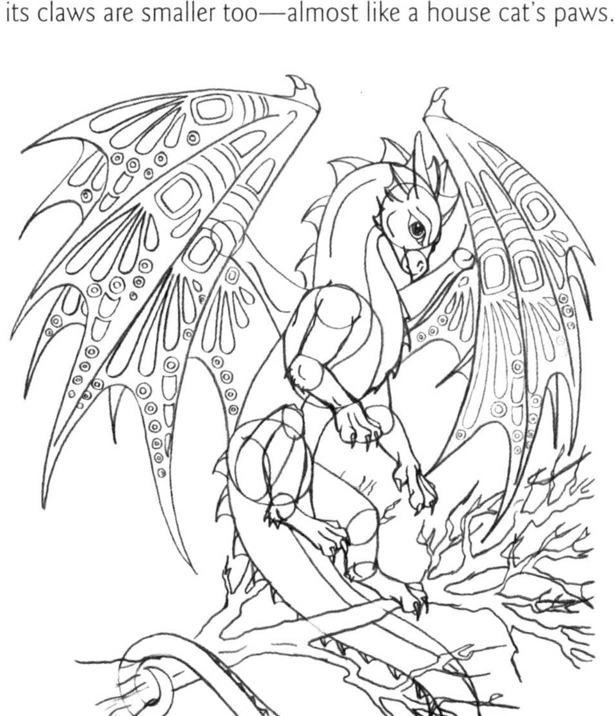

6 Now that the head and claws are done, it's time to fill in the rest of the details. I decided to give this little dragon a butterfly-like pattern to its wings, and because it is already pretty busy looking, I'm not going to draw a pattern on the scales, or even give it belly plates. Add some more branches as well, and try overlapping some over the dragon to give your drawing depth.

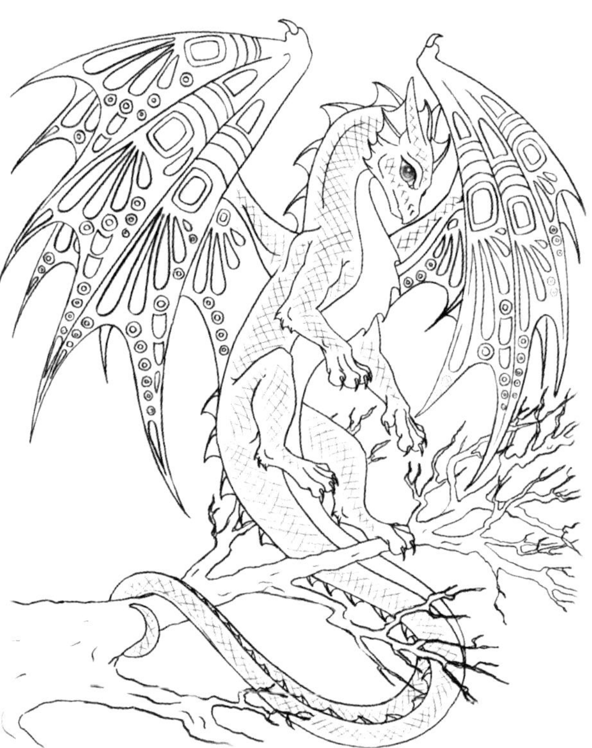

7 Now that all the details have been planned out, the drawing is ready to be cleaned up or copied over to a new piece of paper. Once that's done, add scales to the dragon but remember not to press too hard so you won't dent the paper.

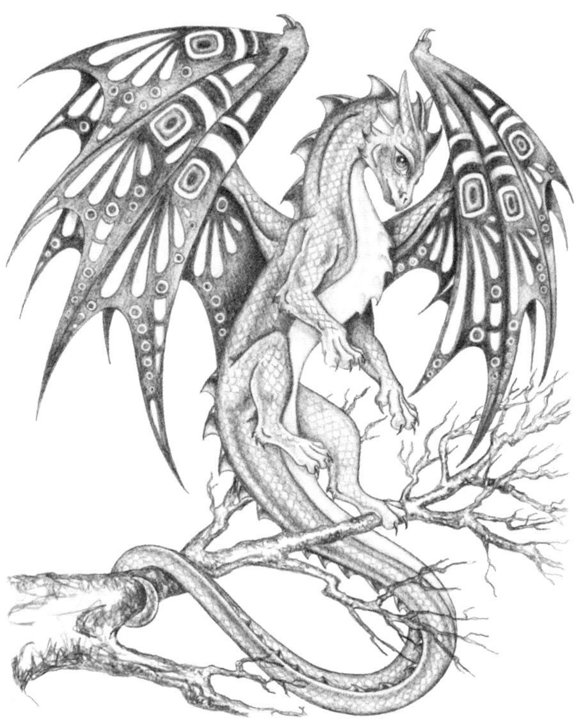

8 On to the shading! I used a B pencil for this first step, and I started with the wings. Don't color in the shapes on the wings; you can use a blending stump to do that next. Round out the scales if you'd like, and start adding shading on the body to add muscle definition.

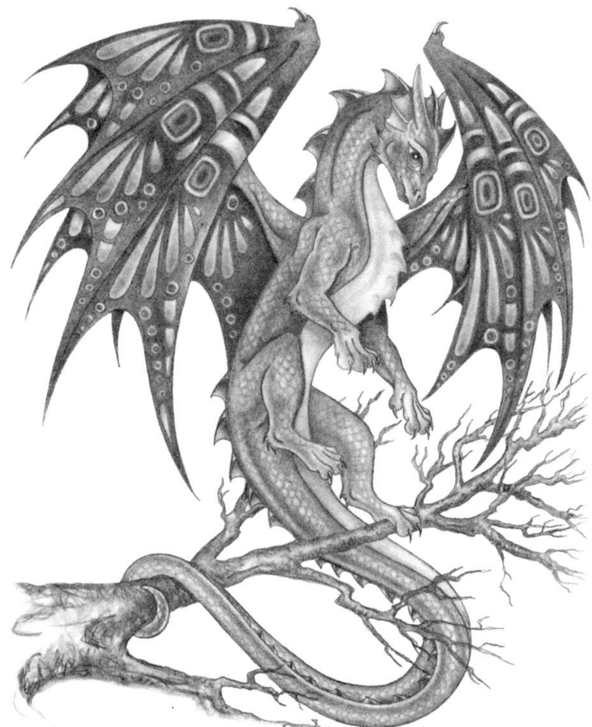

9 Using a very fine-tipped blending stump, carefully blend the wings, making sure not to ruin your pattern. You can shade carefully within some of the shapes on the wings with the blending stump, but make sure you don't press to hard or pull graphite in from the outside of the shape or it will be too dark and look blurry.

10 All done! Once the blending is complete, you can just touch up the drawing to darken areas that need more contrast and use an eraser to lighten areas that might be too dark. Because this dragon is small, you'll want to put it in an environment that shows its size. Drawing leaves, flowers, and buds on the branches, or adding a familiar insect that doesn't vary too much in size, can really help show how big (or little) your dragon is!

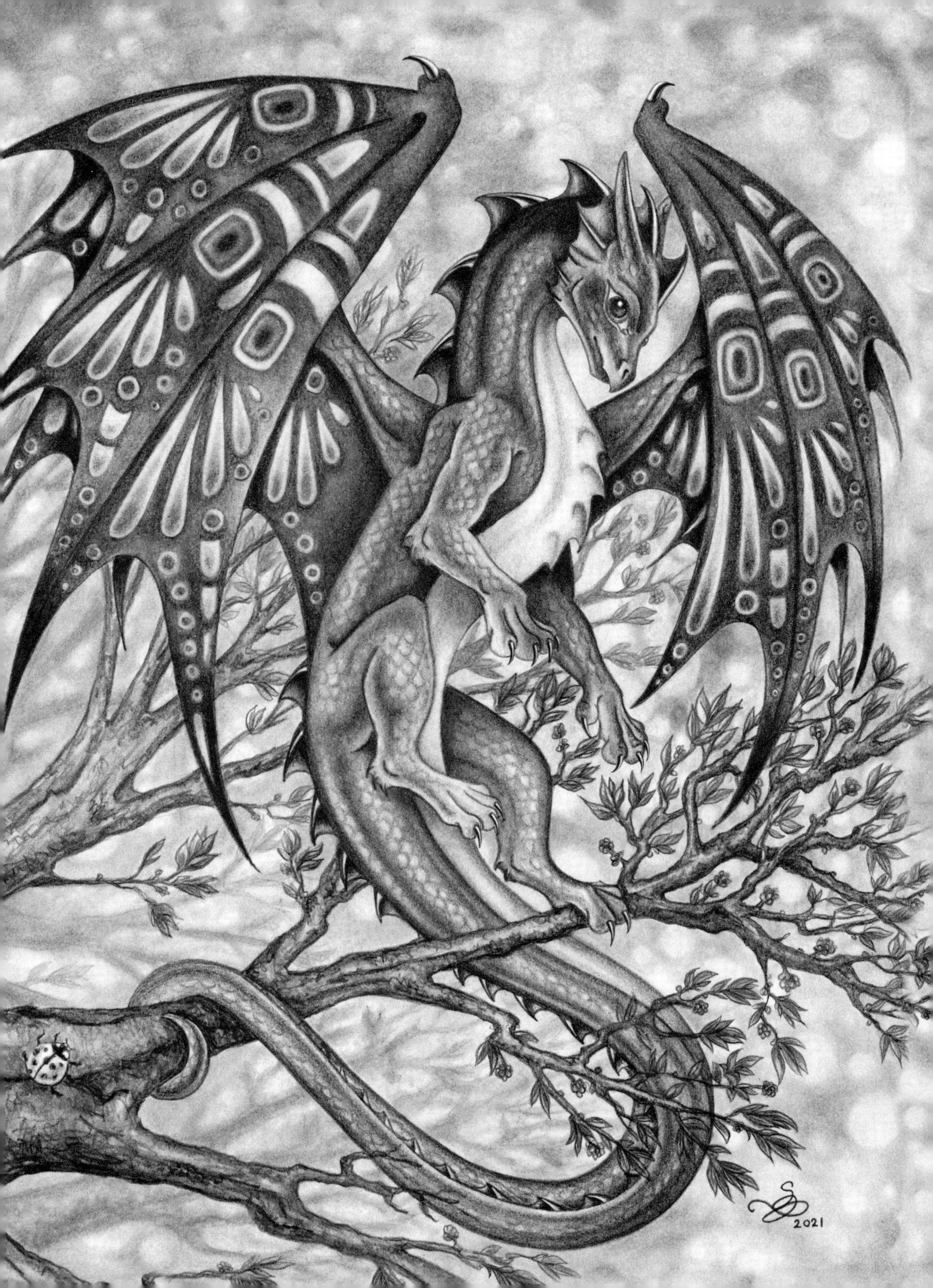
2021

LAST WORDS

Well it looks like our tutorial section has already come to an end! I hope you enjoyed it and found it to be a useful addition to this sketchbook. If you liked the tutorials, feel free to check out my other two drawing books for lots of ideas on how to customize your own fantastic dragons and winged beasts.

In the meantime, keep on drawing! I can't reiterate enough how important practice is. The more you draw, the better you will get. A lot of people have the misconception that in order to be able to draw well you must be born with some sort of innate ability. What a silly idea! You simply need to have the desire to learn how to draw, and the perseverance to keep trying.

Becoming a great artist is the same as becoming a great anything—whether it be a musician, doctor, programmer, or athlete for example—you need to put in the time to learn, practice, and then repeat, repeat, repeat indefinitely! Don't feel discouraged by other artists that you see as being "better" than you—everyone has their own style, so you just need to find yours. Chances are those artists have also put in countless hours and produced lots of pieces they didn't like along the way.

We are all in this artistic journey together, so rather than feeling daunted by other artists' successes, look to them as inspiration and know that you are great as well—and can only get better with time and hard work!

All the best...

Sandra

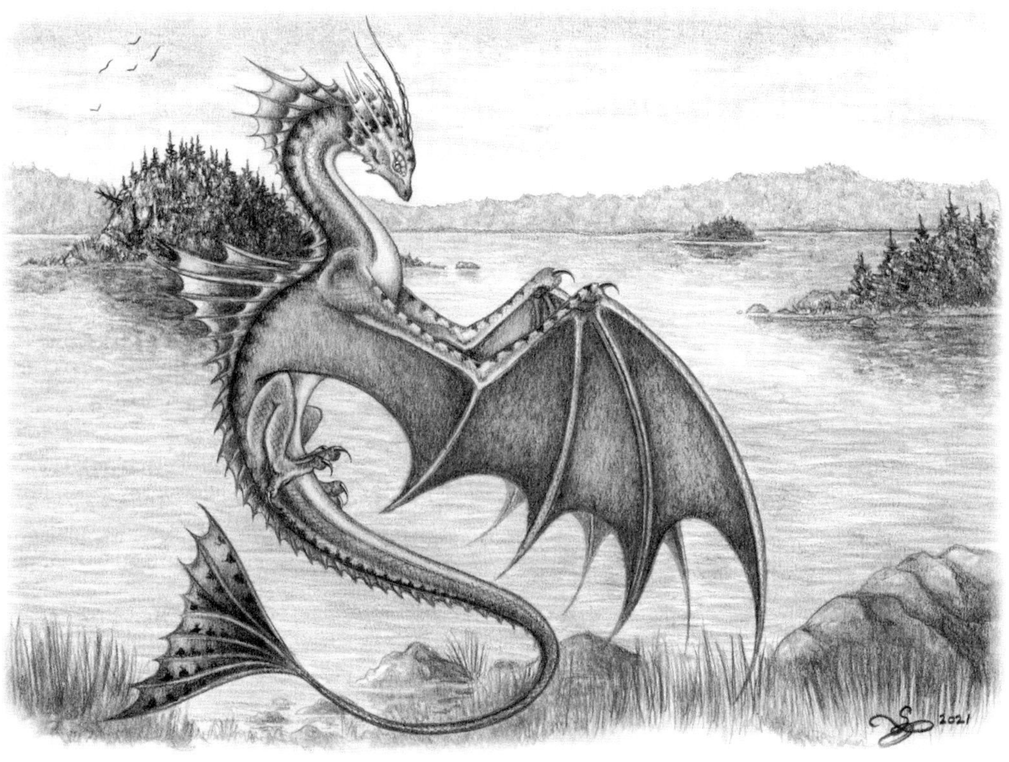

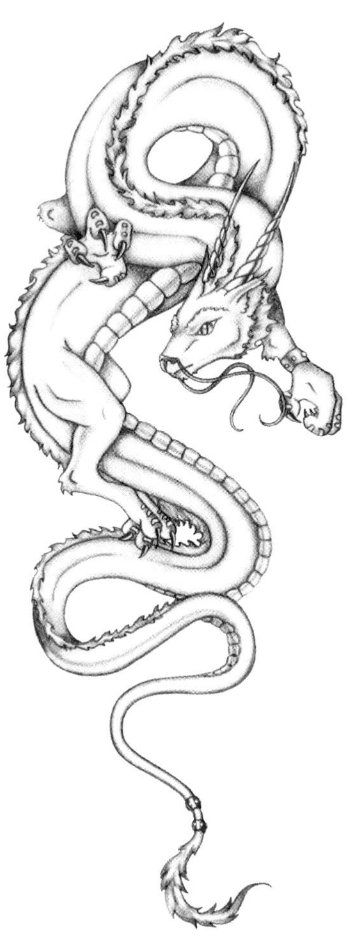

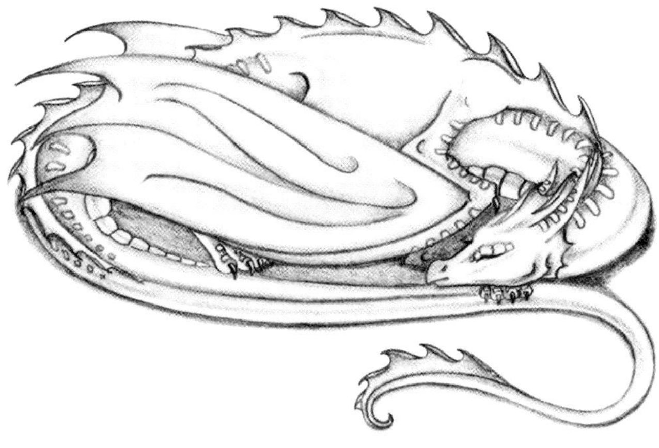

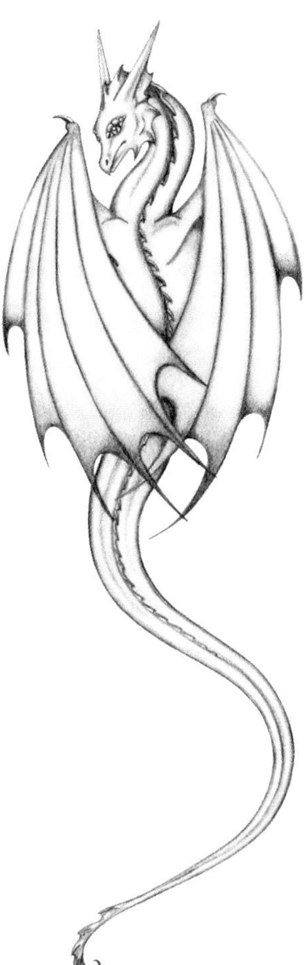

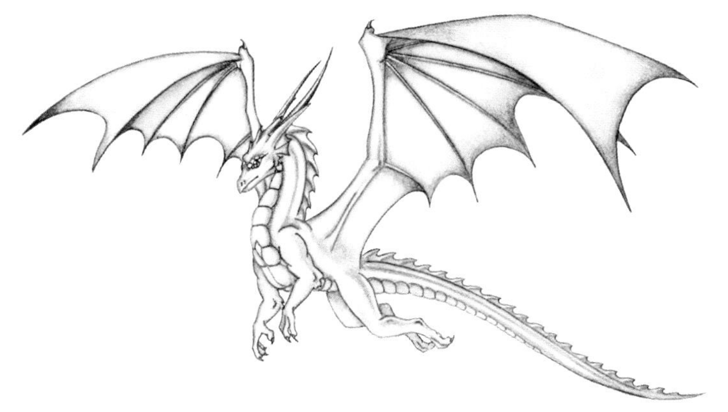

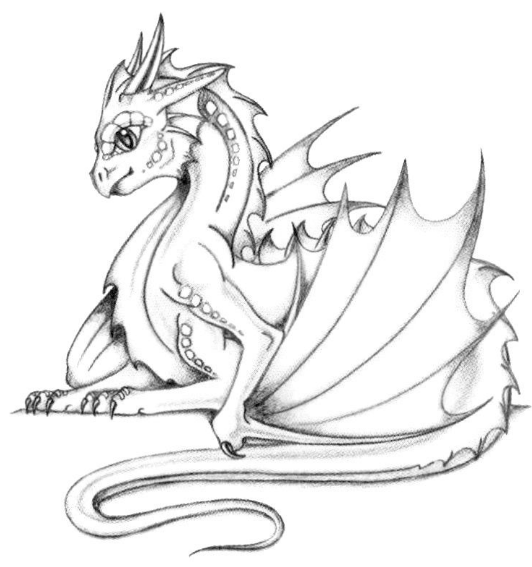

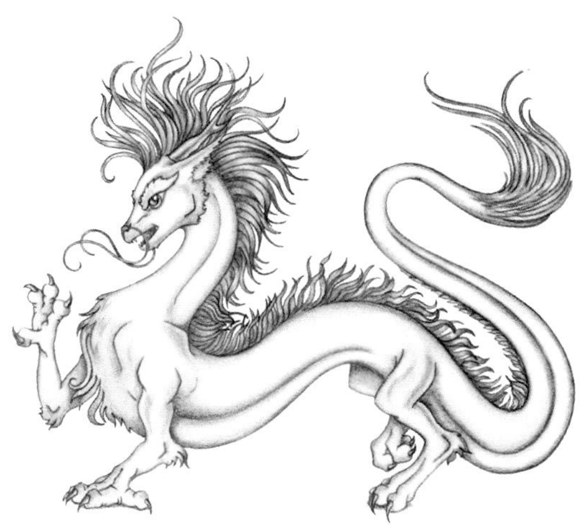

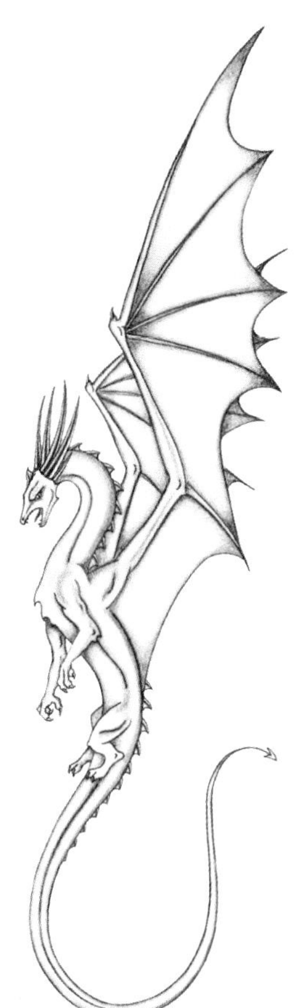

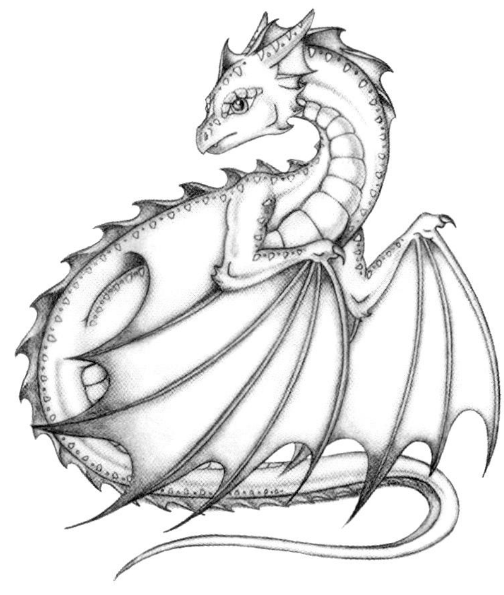

ABOUT THE AUTHOR

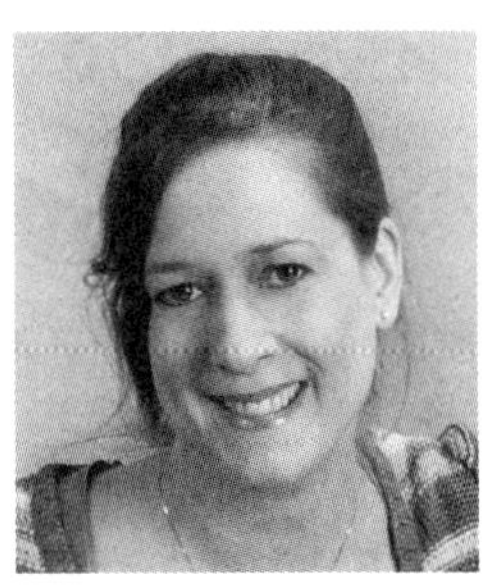

Sandra Staple was born and raised in Halifax, Nova Scotia, where she now lives with her husband, Jason; daughter, Chloe; and son, Logan. Her mother is a local artist, so Sandra has been drawing and painting since she was a young girl, earning distinctions in English and art in high school.

She graduated from Saint Mary's University with a major in computing and information systems, and a minor in creative writing. After graduating, Sandra worked as a business and systems analyst for 17 years before deciding to leave the corporate world to focus on her writing and art.

Sandra's first two drawing books, *Drawing Dragons* and *Drawing Fantastic Dragons*, are both Amazon Number One Best Sellers, and her first book has been featured in Amazon's *Holiday Gift Guide* and *Most Wished For* lists.

Sandra has also managed a very popular web gallery of her art since university, at www.canadiandragon.com. When not drawing or spending time with her family and friends, Sandra can usually be found working in her garden or elbow-deep in her fish tank.

Follow Sandra on Instagram, Facebook, Twitter, and TikTok @SandraStaple for exclusive content, latest work, videos, tutorials, giveaways, and more!

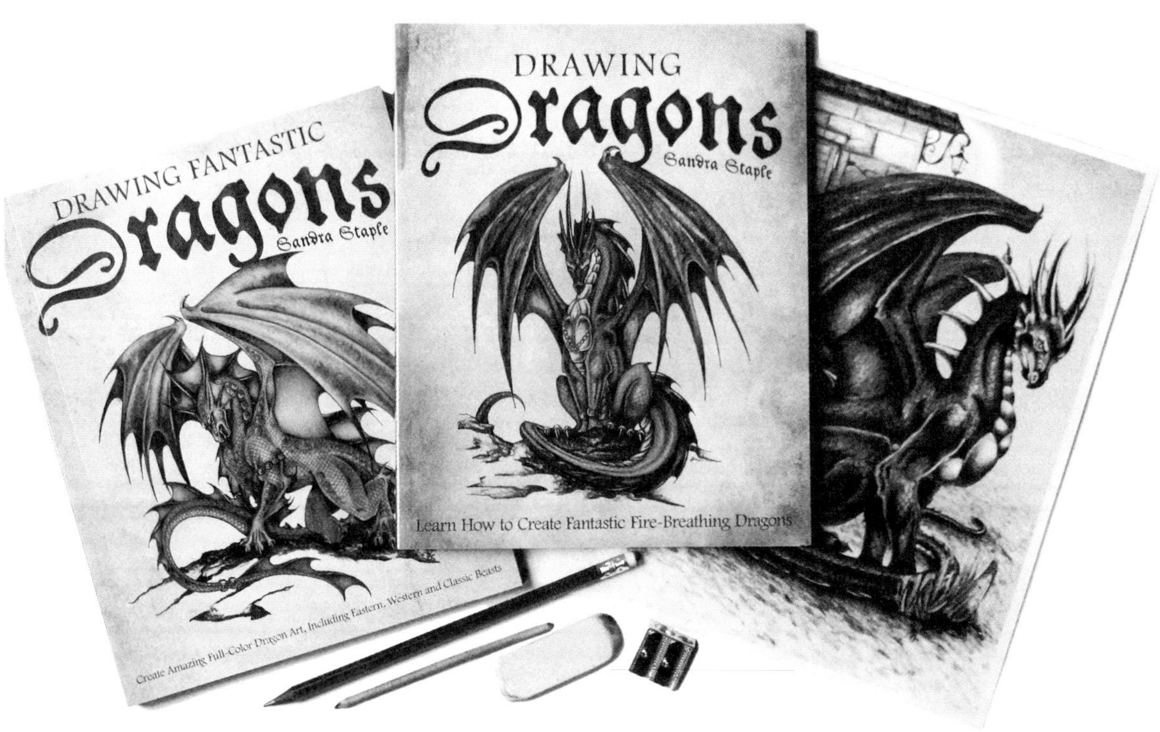